SIDECAR · BACAR

E HAWAIIAN · CASA

DAIQUIRI · FROZEN DAIQUIRI · PAPA

· LONG ISLAND ICED TEA · MAI TAI

MBIE · HURRICANE · BETWEEN THE

PIRINHA · BLUE MARLIN · I DREAM

AIQUIRI · NACIONAL · GREEN FLASH

NDARIN FROM HAVANA · BOSSA NOVA

ODISIAC · ROYAL PALM COCKTAIL

UIRI · VELVET VOODOO · TIDAL WAVE

MAICAN MARTINI · DARK AND STORMY

UDA · JADE · CARIBBEAN FIZZ · · · · ·

Rum Runner - 1½ oz White Rum
4 oz Prune Juice
— over Ice —

Island Breeze 1 oz Coconut Rum
1 oz Mango Rum
1½ oz OJ 1½ oz Cranberry
1 oz . Pineapple Juice
over Ice

Mini Bar *Rum*

Island Suprise :

Mini Bar **Rum**

by MITTIE HELLMICH

photographs by Frankie Frankeny

CHRONICLE BOOKS
SAN FRANCISCO

A huge thanks to the fabulously creative project manager Mary Wruck for her savvy attention to detail, and to the meticulous copy editor Jonathan Kauffman. And a special thanks to Hudson Pierce-Rhoads, Geoffrey Rhoads, and Rick Van Oel.—MH

Library of Congress Cataloging-in-Publication Data available.

ISBN 10: 0-8118-5438-8
ISBN 13: 978-0-8118-5438-2

Manufactured in China.

Drink styling by Alison Richmond
Designed by Hallie Overman, Brooklyn, New York

From Frankie: Thanks to Pamela Geismar and Leslie Jonath.

Distributed in Canada by Raincoast Books
9050 Shaughnessy Street
Vancouver, British Columbia V6P 6E5

10 9 8 7 6 5 4 3 2 1

Chronicle Books LLC
680 Second Street
San Francisco, California 94107

www.chroniclebooks.com

Alizé is a registered trademark of Tradewinds Importing Co., Inc. Angostura bitters is a registered trademark of Angostura International Ltd. Chartreuse is a registered trademark of Chartreuse Corporation. Cointreau is a registered trademark of Cointreau Corporation. Damiana Liqueur is a registered trademark of Damiana Importing, Inc. Frangelico is a registered trademark of C&C International Ltd. Galliano is a registered trademark of Remy Finance B.V. Grand Marnier is a registered trademark of Societe des Produits Marnier-Lapostolle. Kahlúa is a registered trademark of Heaven Hill Distilleries Inc. Pernod is a registered trademark of Pernod Ricard. Tia Maria is a registered trademark of Tia Maria Ltd.

Table of Contents

Introduction

RUM IS A SUGARCANE-BASED LIQUOR with an enveloping warmth and sweet complexity. Literally and figuratively, the spirit of the Caribbean Islands. In 1493, Christopher Columbus was responsible for introducing them to sugarcane, having gathered a few samples in the Canary Islands during his travels. The local islanders soon found quasi-medicinal uses for the fermented cane juice. Around the early 1500s, Portuguese settlers in Brazil discovered that they could distill a spirit from the molasses that would naturally ferment from the heat as it sat in the sugar factories.

Long before whiskey or bourbon gained favor as the first commercially distilled spirit in the colonies, rum was America's spirit of choice. It was made from West Indies molasses acquired through an ignoble practice, which involved the trading of American rum for African slaves and then, in turn, for Caribbean molasses. Rum's notorious reputation for inducing inebriation in American homes sparked the Prohibition movement, led by Carry Nation of the Women's Christian Temperance Union. Nation's infamous yell, "Smash the demon rum!" incited riots of rum-bottle smashing.

But by the 1940s, as cultural attitudes toward rum shifted again, it regained popularity through America's preoccupation with Polynesian exotica. Don the Beachcomber, father of the Zombie and the Scorpion, astutely promoted rum at his Beachcomber bar in Hollywood, offering an extensive cocktail menu that promised exotic island concoctions along with a "cellar" full of hundreds of rums from around the world. Today, we no longer remember its notorious history, steeped in debauchery and politics, and can freely luxuriate in the flavor of rum, which, unlike any other bottled spirit, instantly transports your palate to a balmy place.

The lovely sweetness inherent in the spirit comes from sugarcane, which is boiled down to a rich molasses and then fermented and distilled. It can vary in color, weight, and sweetness, and many nuanced flavors can be found within the various types of rum. In the Caribbean, each island has perfected its distinct style, from the molasses-flavored dark rums of Haiti, Jamaica, and Martinique to the lighter rums of Trinidad, Cuba, Puerto Rico, and the Virgin Islands, which retain very little molasses taste and tend to be drier.

Following is a Rum 101 to help clarify the differing styles:

LIGHT RUMS
Labeled either "white," "light," "silver," or "*blanco*," light rums are clear to pale gold in color, light-bodied, and lightly sweet in flavor, with a dry aroma. To produce lighter varieties of rum, molasses is briefly fermented and usually distilled in a continuous still, then often filtered through charcoal and aged in stainless steel tanks, which add little or no color. With its delicate flavor, this versatile spirit is an excellent choice for most mixed drinks, from coolers to daiquiris.

GOLD RUMS

Labeled "gold" (*oro*) or "amber" (*ambre*), these medium-bodied, smooth rums are basically white rums that have become golden or light brown from aging (from one to three years and up to twelve years) in oak barrels. Gold rums can be used in many cocktails that call for white rum in order to intensify the flavor.

DARK RUMS

Dark rums are robust spirits made in traditional pot stills and further refined through blending with lighter continuous-still-produced spirits. They are aged from three to twelve years in well-charred oak barrels, where they become anywhere from deep gold to dark brown. These dark, full-bodied rums add aggressive flavor to cocktails and are best used to enhance lighter rums in more potent drinks. Many dark rums are excellent for sipping.

AGED, VIEUX, OR AÑEJO RUMS

Similar to good brandies or bourbons, vintage brown rums are aged for at least six years and are meant to be enjoyed like a fine Cognac. Unlike most dark rums, which are heavily flavored, these spirits draw their intensity from a longer aging period. Some connoisseurs search out rare and expensive "single-mark," or unblended, single-batch rums.

SPICED OR FLAVORED RUMS

Spiced or flavored rums, which are growing in popularity, can be made from a base of white, gold, or dark rum that is infused with citrus flavors, vanilla, coconut, pineapple, or other fruits. They are sold as rum liqueurs, bottled rum punches, and rum infusions and bring a new dimension to such classic rum drinks as Daiquiris and Mojitos.

CACHAÇA

Brazil produces cachaça (pronounced *kah-SHAH-suh*), a colorless spirit made from the juice of the first press of unrefined sugarcane, or sometimes from a combination of both molasses and sugarcane juice. Made in pot stills and not aged, cachaça is harsher than rum, with a bite similar to brandy.

OVERPROOF RUMS

Overproof rums, such as Demerara 151 from Guyana or Bacardi 151 from Puerto Rico, are harsh, potent, and flammable. By no means are they meant for drinking straight. Overproof rums are notoriously used to raise the alcohol content of Zombie-like concoctions and are used as the theatrical element in flaming drinks and desserts.

From the mystique of the minty Mojito to the mythologically potent Zombie, the list of legendary drinks made with the pure island alchemy of rum is impressive. The recipes in this book are formulated in reverence to the originals. You'll find drinks that have stood the test of time alongside new urban cocktails that refine the ambrosial flavors of the equatorial latitudes to achieve cosmopolitan perfection. Shake up a few of these tasty rum concoctions and quench your thirst for liquid adventure!

¡Salud!

Glassware, Tools, and Terminology

GLASSWARE

Glassware plays an important role in the much-ritualized cocktail experience. A well-chilled vessel visually entices us with the promise of refreshment, with the right glass adding elegance to even the simplest drink. Glasses come in an endless variety of designs, styles, and colors, but when it comes to setting up your home bar, your repertoire of glassware doesn't have to be extensive to be stylishly appropriate and proficiently functional. A few basic styles—cocktail glasses, highball glasses, old-fashioned and double old-fashioned glasses, champagne flutes, and wineglasses—will see you beautifully through a multitude of drinks.

ESSENTIAL BAR TOOLS

Whether you have a swank bar setup in your favorite entertaining room or an area set aside in the kitchen, you don't need all the high-tech gadgets and gizmos to put together a well-functioning home bar. All you need are the essential bar tools to see you through just about any mixological occasion. You may already have the typical kitchen tools you need: a sharp paring knife for cutting fruit and garnishes, a cutting board for cutting fruit, a bar towel, a good corkscrew and bottle opener, and measuring spoons and cups. To these you may want to add a few of the basic bar tools: a blender with a high-caliber motor, a citrus juicer, a cocktail shaker or a mixing pitcher and stirring rod, a bar spoon, a jigger, an ice bucket and tongs, and, of course, a few cocktail picks and swizzle sticks.

To dash, muddle, top, or float: That is the question. When you want clarification on what exactly that all means or what it means to have a drink served up, neat, straight, or on the rocks, this miniglossary of frequently used bar terms will assist you in navigating bar talk.

· Chaser · The beverage you drink immediately after you have downed anything alcoholic, usually a shot. Typical chasers are beer, club soda, and juice.

· Dash · Either a shake from a bitters bottle or the equivalent of approximately ⅛ teaspoon.

· Dry · A term meaning "not sweet," used either in reference to some wines or to describe nonsweet spirits or cocktails, such as a Dry Martini, which uses dry vermouth rather than sweet vermouth.

· Float · This describes the technique of slowly pouring a small amount of spirit (usually a liqueur or cream) over the surface of a drink so that it floats, or sits atop another liquid without mixing. The customary technique is to slowly pour the liquid over the back of a spoon.

· Highball · The main characteristics of a highball drink are that it has two ingredients—one spirit and one mixer, usually carbonated, poured into a tall, narrow glass filled with ice (the shape of the glass helps to contain the carbonation)—and that it can be mixed quickly. The tall, but narrower Collins glass is a frequent alternative to the highball glass.

· Lowball · A lowball is any drink served with ice in a short glass, such as an old-fashioned glass.

· Muddle · A technique that involves using a small wooden "muddler" or spoon to mash fruits or herbs in the bottom of a glass, usually together with bitters or sugar, to release their aromatic flavors.

· Neat · Describes a single spirit or liqueur served in a glass "straight up"—enjoyed on its own, unchilled, and without ice, water, or any other ingredients.

· Neutral Spirit · A spirit distilled from grain to produce a virtually tasteless, colorless alcohol that is 95.5 percent ABV (alcohol by volume) and is used as a base for spirits such as vodka or gin or for blending with straight whiskeys or other spirits and liqueurs.

· On the Rocks · A term used to describe any liquor or mixed drink served over ice—the "rocks" being ice cubes—as opposed to a drink served "up" (without ice).

· Perfect · A term used to describe specific cocktails that contain equal parts dry and sweet vermouth, as in a Perfect Manhattan or Perfect Martini.

· Pousse-café · Literally translated as the "coffee-pusher" (and pronounced *poos-caf-FAY*), this after-dinner drink features colorful strata of liqueurs, syrups, spirits, and creams in a stemmed glass. The multiple layers—as many as seven—are artfully floated one on top of another so that each stratum remains separate. The heaviest liquid goes in first, the lightest is added last.

· Proof · A legal measurement of the alcoholic strength of a spirit. In the United States, proof is calculated thusly: 1 degree of proof equals 0.5 percent ABV (alcohol by volume). Therefore, a spirit labeled "80 proof" is 40 percent ABV, a 100-proof spirit is 50 percent ABV, and so on.

· Splash · A small amount that can fall anywhere between a dash and about an ounce, depending on who's doing the splashing.

· Straight · This term describes a spirit served without any other liquor or mixers, either poured into a chilled glass or over ice, occasionally with the addition of a splash of club soda or water.

· Top or Top Off · A term used by bartenders to describe the act of pouring the last ingredient into a drink, usually club soda or ginger ale, filling to the top of the glass. Also used to describe filling a beer mug from a tap.

· Up · Describes a drink served without ice in a cocktail glass. Usually the drink is shaken in a cocktail shaker and strained "up" into a chilled cocktail glass, as opposed to "on the rocks," which means served over ice.

simple

Easy-to-prepare cocktails with four ingredients or less

Cuba Libre

CUBA LIBRE MEANS "FREE CUBA." As cocktail lore tells it, the name of this cocktail was coined by an American soldier who was stationed in Cuba during the Spanish-American War to assist the island in its liberation from Spain. Although many people think of the Cuba Libre as a sweet drink that appeals to younger tastes, when it is made correctly—with lots of fresh lime juice—the sweetness of the cola is refreshingly counterbalanced. Mix up a few for friends, and free the Cuba Libre from its bad reputation!

½ lime
2 ounces light rum
3 to 4 ounces chilled cola
lime wedge

Squeeze the lime half into an ice-filled highball glass and drop it in. Add the rum, top with cola, and stir. Garnish with the lime wedge.

Florida Special

A COCKTAIL WITH A SWANK AND SUNNY DISPOSITION, the Florida Special is made with the complex fruit flavors of sour-cherry-flavored maraschino liqueur, orange liqueur, and a refreshing splash of fresh orange juice.

1 1/2 ounces gold rum
1/4 ounce triple sec
1/4 ounce maraschino liqueur
1/4 ounce fresh orange juice

Shake the ingredients vigorously with ice. Strain into a chilled cocktail glass.

Cuban Sidecar

YOU SIMPLY CAN'T GO WRONG WITH THIS SULTRY LATIN TWIST on the sidecar, a classic mixological triangulation of rich spirits with sweet orange liqueur and tart lime.

1 ounce light rum
1 ounce Cointreau
1 ounce fresh lime juice
Lime twist

Shake the liquid ingredients vigorously with ice. Strain into a chilled cocktail glass. Twist the lime peel over the drink, and drop it in.

Bacardi Cocktail

A RUM CLASSIC THAT PUTS A SPIN ON THE DAIQUIRI by replacing the simple syrup with grenadine. The Bacardi Cocktail is the only cocktail protected by a court ruling: In 1936, a New York court ruled that it must be made with Bacardi rum—but when made behind closed doors, any light rum will do.

Shake the liquid ingredients vigorously with ice. Strain into a chilled cocktail glass. Garnish with the maraschino cherry.

2 ounces Bacardi light or
gold rum
1 ounce fresh lime juice
½ ounce grenadine
Maraschino cherry

Bay Breeze

NEW ENGLAND MEETS THE ISLANDS in this refreshing, tropical take on the quintessential summer highball.

Pour the ingredients into an ice-filled highball glass and stir.

2 ounces light rum
3 ounces cranberry juice
1 ounce pineapple juice

Rum and Tonic

THE CLASSIC SUMMER COMBO GOES TO THE BEACH and gets a
splash of equatorial spirits. This drink is at its best when made
with a good-quality dark rum from Jamaica, Bermuda, or Haiti.

2 ounces dark rum
4 to 6 ounces chilled tonic
water
Lime wedge

Pour the liquid ingredients into an
ice-filled highball glass. Stir well. Run
the lime wedge around the rim,
squeeze it over the drink, and drop
it in.

Bolero

THIS AROMATIC RUM MARTINI gets a splash of sophistication
from Calvados, the fine apple brandy made in Normandy, France.
If you don't feel like splurging on a high-end aged Calvados,
purchase a younger one. Applejack, the American version, also
makes a good, economical alternative.

1½ ounces light rum
¾ ounce Calvados
(or applejack)
¼ teaspoon sweet vermouth

Stir the ingredients in a mixing
glass with ice. Strain into a chilled
cocktail glass.

savvy

· Essential recipes for every bartender ·

Blue Hawaiian

YOU JUST CAN'T ESCAPE THE IMAGE OF ELVIS crooning over some turquoise lagoon while sipping this blue-hued elixir. Its wave of tiki flavors is sure to hit your senses like a Technicolor movie.

Shake the liquid ingredients vigorously with ice. Strain into an ice-filled highball glass. Garnish with the pineapple and cherry.

1 ounce light rum
1 ounce blue curaçao
1 ounce cream of coconut
2 ounces pineapple juice
Pineapple wedge
Maraschino cherry

Casablanca

ENVISION THIS STYLISH LITTLE NUMBER being shaken and served at Rick's Cafe as the sparks fly between Bogart and Bergman. The meeting of orange, sour cherry, and lime with the mellow sweetness of light rum makes for perfect chemistry.

Shake the ingredients vigorously with ice. Strain into a chilled cocktail glass.

2¼ ounces light rum
½ ounce Cointreau
½ ounce maraschino liqueur
½ ounce fresh lime juice

Bahama Mama

THE BAHAMAN ART OF RELAXING includes sipping a tropical concoction while enjoying a spectacular sunset, and this potent libation certainly fills the bill. It's packed with all the essential flavors of the islands: dark rum, pineapple juice, coconut, and coffee (I prefer Tia Maria, the coffee-flavored liqueur from Jamaica). One last little touch—a high-octane float of 151-proof rum—will *really* get you relaxed.

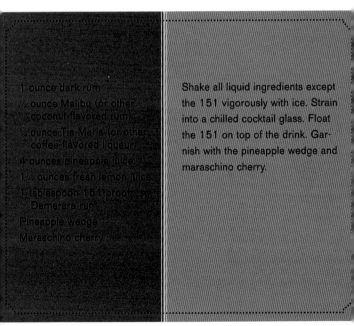

1 ounce dark rum

½ ounce Malibu (or other coconut-flavored rum)

½ ounce Tia Maria (or other coffee-flavored liqueur)

4 ounces pineapple juice

1½ ounces fresh lemon juice

1 tablespoon 151-proof Demerara rum

Pineapple wedge

Maraschino cherry

Shake all liquid ingredients except the 151 vigorously with ice. Strain into a chilled cocktail glass. Float the 151 on top of the drink. Garnish with the pineapple wedge and maraschino cherry.

Scorpion

THIS POTENT CONCOCTION IS A FAUX POLYNESIAN CLASSIC from the South Seas–infatuated 1950s. It owes its existence to Don the Beachcomber, the father of tiki mixology. A close cousin to the Mai Tai and the Zombie, the Scorpion was frequently served in a huge communal tiki bowl, enough for four patrons, and bedecked with gardenias and long straws. This recipe conveniently serves one—and flowers are optional.

Shake the liquid ingredients vigorously with ice. Strain into a large ice-filled wineglass. Garnish with the skewered pineapple and maraschino cherry, and float the flower on top, if using.

2 ounces light or gold rum
¾ ounce brandy
½ ounce dry vermouth
1½ ounces fresh orange juice
1¼ ounces fresh lemon juice
½ ounce orgeat
  (or almond-flavored syrup)
Pineapple spear
Maraschino cherry
Edible flower (such as
  orange blossom, gardenia,
  or nasturtium), optional

Daiquiri

ACCORDING TO LEGEND, around the late 1890s, an American engineer by the name of Jennings Cox ran out of gin while entertaining in Daiquiri, a remote village in Cuba. Forced to improvise, Cox came up with this now-classic rum-based concoction. Given the status of rum as the highly esteemed "milk of Cuba," however, it's likely that this combination had been enjoyed before.

Havana soon became the daiquiri mecca. The undisputed headquarters of the drink was the El Floridita bar, where legendary bartender Constantino Ribailagua introduced a frozen version. His special method of straining the drink after blending it with crushed ice avoided further dilution while retaining the frosty character of the drink, elevating the daiquiri to perfection.

In its original form, the daiquiri is simple yet sublime, blending the delicate sweetness of rum with sugar and the juice of one lime. The secret to making a perfect daiquiri is not just in the balance of ingredients: You must also squeeze the lime with your fingers to allow the oils from the rind to mingle with the juice, intensifying its flavor. Always use fresh lime juice! To use lime juice concentrate in a daiquiri would be an unthinkable travesty.

The classic daiquiri is also a great base for improvisation. Embellish it with your favorite fruit or substitute dark, aged, or spiced rums and really push the limits.

Classic Daiquiri

TO MAKE THE CLASSIC DAQUIRI, following tradition, shake with Bacardi white rum and the juice of half a lime.

Shake the liquid ingredients vigorously with ice. Strain into a chilled cocktail glass. Garnish with the lime slice.

2 ounces light rum
1 ounce fresh lime juice
¼ ounce simple syrup (page 13) or 1 teaspoon superfine sugar
lime slice

Frozen Daiquiri

WHEN SUMMER TEMPERATURES REACH A SWELTERING HIGH, the favorite Cuban libation to cool things down is this frosty daiquiri, based on El Floridita's recipe.

Combine ingredients in a blender with ½ cup cracked ice. Blend until smooth. Pour into a chilled cocktail glass, and serve with a straw.

2 ounces white rum
½ ounce fresh lime juice
½ ounce simple syrup (page 13) or 1 teaspoon superfine sugar
dash of maraschino liquor

· Variations · By simply adding your favorite fresh or frozen fruit to the Frozen Daiquiri recipe, you can create delicious tropical ambrosias. Many prefer to add a dash or two of dark rum for added richness. The following are a few luscious fruit daiquiri suggestions:

For a FROZEN WATERMELON DAIQUIRI, add 1 cup seeded, cubed watermelon and ¼ cup lime sorbet.

For a DAIQUIRI DE PIÑA, add ½ cup cubed pineapple.

For a PEACH DAIQUIRI, add ½ cup fresh peach slices and ½ ounce peach brandy.

For a STRAWBERRY DAIQUIRI, add ½ cup sliced strawberries and ¼ ounce crème de framboise.

For a BANANA DAIQUIRI, add ½ cup sliced ripe banana and ¼ ounce crème de banane, or another banana liqueur.

· Basic Simple Syrup · Also known as SUGAR SYRUP, this is an essential ingredient in many drinks, as it requires no dissolving or excessive stirring to incorporate, unlike granulated sugar. Makes 2 cups.

1 cup water   2 cups sugar

In a small saucepan, bring the water to a boil. Remove the pan from the heat and add the sugar. Stir until the sugar is completely dissolved. Cool completely before using or refrigerating. Pour into a clean glass jar, cap tightly, and store (indefinitely) in the refrigerator until needed.

Papa Hemingway's Daiquiri

ALSO KNOWN UNDER VARIOUS ALIASES, including Papa Doble or Ernest Hemingway Special, this legendary concoction fueled the literary imagination of Ernest Hemingway. "Papa" preferred his favorite Cuban cocktail cold and sour, without sugar and with twice as much rum as the traditional daiquiri. This distinctive daiquiri was created for Hemingway by Ribailagua at El Floridita. If you prefer a lighter, sweeter variation, use 2 ounces of rum and add a teaspoon of superfine sugar, which permits more of the grapefruit and sour-cherry flavors to shine through. Living in Cuba during Prohibition, Hemingway could indulge in Havana Club Silver Dry rum, and if you can get ahold of a bottle while overseas, you'll be able to experience this drink in its purest form.

Combine the liquid ingredients in a blender with ½ cup ice. Blend until smooth. Pour into a chilled cocktail glass. Squeeze the lime wedge over the drink and drop it in.

3 ounces rum
½ ounce maraschino liqueur
1½ ounces fresh grapefruit juice
¾ ounce fresh lime juice
1 lime wedge

Presidente

HERE IS A FAVORED, TRADITIONAL DRINK HAILING FROM CUBA.
Complementing rum with a perfect balance of sweet and dry
vermouths and a dash of orange essence, the Presidente has all
the credentials and panache of a fine martini-esque cocktail.

1½ ounces light rum
½ ounce dry vermouth
½ ounce sweet vermouth
¼ ounce triple sec
Orange twist
Maraschino cherry

Stir the liquid ingredients in a
mixing glass with ice. Strain into a
chilled cocktail glass. Run the
orange peel around the rim, twist it
over the drink, and drop it in,
along with the maraschino cherry.

· Variation · For an EL PRESIDENTE, add ¼ ounce fresh lemon juice
and a dash of grenadine, sans garnishes.

Long Island Iced Tea

SOME PURISTS CLAIM YOU SHOULD NEVER MIX VODKA AND GIN TOGETHER, but this potent classic defies many taboos, and indeed tastes dangerously like iced tea.

Pour all of the liquid ingredients except the cola into an ice-filled collins glass. Top with cola and stir gently. Squeeze the lemon wedge into the drink and drop it in.

Ice cubes with a pick
¾ ounce gin
¾ ounce vodka
¾ ounce tequila
¾ ounce Cointreau
(or triple sec)
1 ounce fresh lime juice
¾ ounce 151-proof rum
2 to 3 ounces chilled cola
Lemon wedge

· Variations · For a MIAMI ICED TEA, substitute blue curaçao for the Cointreau.

For a NEW ENGLAND ICED TEA, add 1 ounce simple syrup (page 28) or 1 tablespoon superfine sugar and substitute cranberry juice for the cola.

Mai Tai

ONE OF THE TRUE VETERANS OF THE TROPICAL DRINK GENRE. The following is the original Trader Vic's recipe from 1944. When made with the classic ingredients, it lives up to its archetypal roots, and deserves its Tahitian title, which means "out of this world." *Rhum vieux* from Martinique is the ideal component, but given its scarcity in the States, any aged (añejo) rum will work just as well.

Shake the liquid ingredients vigorously with ice. Strain into an ice-filled collins glass or large wineglass. Garnish with the orange blossom and orange spiral.

- 1½ ounces Myers's Original Dark (or other dark Jamaican rum)
- 1 ounce Martinique *rhum vieux* (or other aged rum)
- ½ ounce orange curaçao
- ¼ ounce simple syrup (page 28) or ½ teaspoon superfine sugar
- ½ ounce orgeat (or almond-flavored syrup)
- 1¼ ounces fresh lime juice
- ½ ounce fresh orange juice
- Orange blossom (or tiny purple orchid)
- Orange peel spiral

Piña Colada

THIS LUSCIOUS PUERTO RICAN CLASSIC FROM THE 1950s, purportedly invented by bartender Ramón "Monchito" Marrero at the Caribe Hilton in San Juan made its way into the tropical cocktail repertoire and gained extreme popularity by the 1970s. The phrase *piña colada* literally means "strained pineapple." In fact, inspiration for the drink comes in a can: the sweet, sweet viscous coconut cream known as Coco Lopez.

2 ounces Puerto Rican
    light rum
6 ounces pineapple juice
2 ounces coconut cream
Pineapple spear
Maraschino cherry

Shake the liquid ingredients vigorously with ice. Strain into a large ice-filled wineglass. Garnish with the pineapple spear and maraschino cherry.

· Variation · For a deluxe spin on the classic Piña Colada, the COLADA NUEVA, add 1 ounce Alizé de France passion fruit liqueur, ½ cup diced fresh pineapple, 1½ ounces mango juice or nectar, and ½ ounce fresh lime juice. Combine in a blender with 1 cup of ice, and blend until smooth.

Planter's Punch

THE ORIGINS OF THIS CLASSIC ARE HARD TO PIN DOWN. Some cocktail lore names the Myers's rum company in Jamaica as the source, while other stories credit a bartender at the Planter's House Hotel in St. Louis in the mid to late 1800s. While plenty of versions claim to be the original, my only claim about this recipe is that it's a great one. For a bit of effervescence, you may wish to add a splash of club soda.

Shake the liquid ingredients vigorously with ice. Strain into an ice-filled highball glass. Garnish with the orange slice and maraschino cherry.

2 ounces dark rum
1 ounce light rum
1½ ounces fresh orange juice
1½ ounces pineapple juice
½ ounce fresh lime juice
½ ounce simple syrup
 (6 to 7.5 ml) ½ teaspoon
 superfine sugar
 dash of grenadine
 orange slice
 Maraschino cherry

· Variation · For a WEST INDIAN PUNCH, add ¾ ounce crème de banane or other banana liqueur, omit the simple syrup and grenadine, and dust the top with freshly grated or ground nutmeg.

Zombie

DON THE BEACHCOMBER'S MIND-ALTERING CONCOCTION has been subject to variation since its conception in 1934, but this recipe loyally adheres to the original, combining three types of rum—light, gold, and dark—a blend of fresh fruit juices—and the classic finishing touch—a float of 151-proof rum on top. Deceptively smooth, this glass of velvet dynamite deserves Don's house rule of "only two per customer."

1 ounce light Puerto Rican rum

1 ounce gold (añejo) rum

1 ounce dark Jamaican rum

½ ounce apricot brandy

1 ounce crème de banane

1 ounce pineapple juice

1 ounce fresh lemon juice

1 ounce fresh lime juice

¼ ounce grenadine

1 tablespoon brown sugar

½ ounce 151-proof Demerara rum

Shake all liquid ingredients but the 151 vigorously with ice. Strain into an ice-filled 16-ounce chilled zombie glass (or large chilled red-wine glass). Float the 151 on the top of the drink.

NOTE: Garnish with a skewer of fresh fruit and edible flowers, if desired.

Hurricane

THE ORIGINAL HURRICANE, created in the 1940s at Pat O'Brien's in New Orleans, was a super-potent concoction that almost doubles the rum of this version—4½ ounces to be exact—served over ice in a hurricane glass. If you wish to attempt the classic formula, you might also need a lamppost to hold on to.

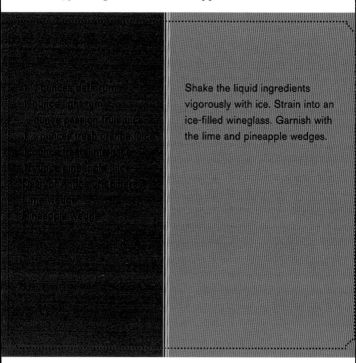

1½ ounces dark rum
1 ounce light rum
½ ounce passion fruit juice
1½ ounces fresh orange juice
1 ounce fresh lime juice
1 ounce pineapple juice
Dash of Angostura bitters
Lime wedge
Pineapple wedge

Shake the liquid ingredients vigorously with ice. Strain into an ice-filled wineglass. Garnish with the lime and pineapple wedges.

Between the Sheets

IN THIS CLASSIC COCKTAIL FROM THE 1920s, a balmy breeze
of Demerara rum warms up a good Cognac to make one
smooth-as-silk aphrodisiac. Who knows, it might just lead you …
hence, the name.

Rub the rim of a chilled cocktail
glass with the lemon wedge
and rim with sugar. Shake the liquid
ingredients vigorously with
ice. Strain into the prepared glass.
Garnish with the lemon twist.

Lemon wedge
Superfine sugar
¾ ounce Demerara
    (or spiced rum)
¾ ounce Cognac (or brandy)
¾ ounce Grand Marnier
½ ounce fresh lemon juice
Lemon twist

Mojito

HAVANA'S REFRESHING ANSWER TO THE MINT JULEP has become a new standard in many American hot spots. Mojitos are traditionally made by muddling together mint, lime, and sugar, ideally with a white rum. Some versions add a splash of club soda. Here are two different ways to prepare the Mojito. One is the traditional method; the other is a quicker version that takes the "shaken, not stirred" route to Havana.

1 ounce fresh lime juice

1 tablespoon superfine sugar

6 to 8 fresh mint leaves

2 ounces light rum

3 to 4 ounces chilled club soda

Fresh mint sprig

TRADITIONAL: In the bottom of a highball glass, muddle together the lime juice, sugar, and mint leaves until the sugar is dissolved. Add the rum. Fill the glass with ice and top with club soda. Garnish with the mint sprig.

SHAKEN: Shake the lime juice, sugar, mint leaves, and rum vigorously with ice. Without straining, pour the entire contents of the shaker into a highball glass, and top with club soda. Garnish with the mint sprig.

Yellow Bird

THIS CARIBBEAN FAVORITE beautifully brings together light
and dark rums with citrus juices and a hint of coffee-flavored
Tia Maria from Jamaica for a powerful punch of island flavors.
Another popular version substitutes ½ ounce Galliano and
½ ounce Cointreau for the Tia Maria and orange juice.

Shake the liquid ingredients
vigorously with ice. Strain
into a chilled highball glass.
Garnish with the mint sprig
and maraschino cherry.

1 ounce dark rum
1 ounce light rum
½ ounce Tia Maria
1½ ounces fresh orange juice
1 ounce fresh lime juice
Fresh mint sprig
Maraschino cherry

Caipirinha

THIS BRAZILIAN CLASSIC IS TRADITIONALLY MADE WITH CACHAÇA, the fiery Brazilian spirit with a distinctive bite. The name (pronounced *kye-pee-REEN-ya*), loosely translates as "country bumpkin" or "little peasant girl," referring to its "uncivilized" preparation in the same glass from which it will be sipped. As you muddle lime wedges against granulated sugar in the bottom of a heavy glass, the crushed peels release their fragrant oils.

2 teaspoons sugar or
superfine sugar
4 or 5 lime wedges
2 ounces cachaça

Muddle the sugar and lime wedges together in an old-fashioned glass until the sugar is dissolved and the lime juice is released. Fill the glass with ice and pour in the cachaça. Stir briefly.

· Variations · Add a few pieces of fruit, such as raspberries, blueberries, or strawberries, to muddle with the lime wedges.

· A few new favorite cachaça cocktails from Brazilian hot spots ·
For a SPICED MANDARIN CAIPIRINHA, add a mandarin orange wedge and cinnamon to the muddled ingredients, and add ½ ounce Mandarine Napoléon liqueur with the cachaça.

For a CAIPITETRA, add mint to the muddled ingredients, and add 1 ounce fresh orange juice with the cachaça.

· sophisticated ·

· A little more work but definitely worth the effort ·

Blue Marlin

INTRIGUED BY THE MIXOLOGICAL POSSIBILITIES of lemon-flavored rum and the sweet orange flavor of blue curaçao, I came up with this citrusy, sugar-dusted, aquamarine potion, which laps at the sides of your cocktail glass like an incoming tide.

Rub the rim of a chilled cocktail glass with the lemon wedge and rim with sugar. Shake the liquid ingredients vigorously with ice. Strain into the prepared glass. Float the orange blossom on top of the drink.

Lemon wedge
Sugar
2 ounces citron rum
¾ ounce blue curaçao
½ ounce sweet-and-sour (recipe follows)
Orange blossom

· Sweet-and-Sour · Citrus is an essential ingredient in many drinks, and recipes frequently call for the classic sweet-and-sour mixture that cuts to the chase and covers both your sweet and citrus flavor needs. Makes 2½ cups.

½ cup cooled simple syrup (page 28)

¾ cup fresh lime juice

¾ cup fresh lemon juice

¼ cup water

Pour all the ingredients into a clean glass jar, with a tight-fitting lid. Close the lid tightly, and shake the contents together until well mixed. Refrigerate until needed or for up to 10 days.

I Dream of Jeanie Martini

THIS DELECTABLE COCKTAIL simply insists it be let out of
the bottle and shaken. It has a mischievous, sassy tang and a
magical balance of sweet, sour, citrus, and fruity flavors.
Straight from the Beauty Bar, a Manhattan hot spot, the drink
was conjured by master mixologist Lara Turchinsky.

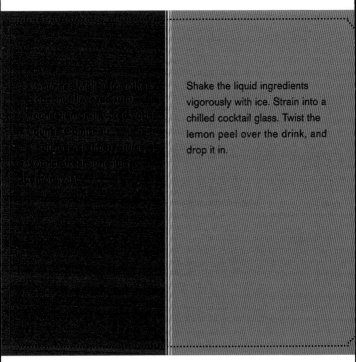

2 ounces Melini (or other
coconut-flavored rum)

1 ounce lemon-flavored vodka

1 ounce Cointreau

½ ounce sweet-and-sour

½ ounce cranberry juice

Lemon twist

Shake the liquid ingredients
vigorously with ice. Strain into a
chilled cocktail glass. Twist the
lemon peel over the drink, and
drop it in.

Guavalicious Daiquiri

TEMPTED TO PUT AN EXOTIC SPIN ON THE DAIQUIRI, I've paired sweet guava nectar with honey, melon, strawberries, the buttery warmth of Barbancourt rum, and a delicate lime tang. They come together beautifully in this pink-hued flower of a drink that's pleasantly reminiscent of pink grapefruit.

Shake the liquid ingredients and sugar vigorously with ice. Strain into a chilled cocktail glass. Garnish with the lime peel spiral

2 ounces rum (Barbancourt)
1 ounce guava nectar
½ ounce fresh lime juice
1 teaspoon honey
lime peel spiral

Nacional

THIS SUBLIME GOLD-RUM COCKTAIL is warmed with apricot brandy and pineapple, lending a subtle fruitiness; a little lime juice adds the perfect amount of zing.

Shake the ingredients vigorously with ice. Strain into a chilled cocktail glass.

1½ ounces gold rum
½ ounce apricot brandy
½ ounce pineapple juice
½ ounce fresh lime juice

Green Flash

AS SOUTH PACIFIC LEGEND HAS IT, on cloudless evenings, an ephemeral moment called the "green flash" occurs: Just as the sun goes down, a green glow appears along the horizon for 2 or 3 seconds. This dazzling moment has inspired many a tropical green concoction, and I just couldn't resist getting in on the act. My own beachcomber's rendition is a refreshing rum fizz laced with the herbal notes of green Chartreuse, which imparts a flavor reminiscent of a Gin and Tonic and lends the drink a celadon-hued glow.

1½ ounces silver rum
¼ ounce green Chartreuse
½ ounce fresh lime juice
1 tablespoon superfine sugar
2 to 3 ounces chilled club soda
1 lime wedge

Shake the rum, Chartreuse, lime juice, and superfine sugar vigorously with ice. Strain into an ice-filled highball glass. Top with club soda and stir gently. Squeeze the lime wedge over the drink, and drop it in.

Acapulco

A DRINK THAT EPITOMIZES THE GLITZ of Mexico's famous oceanside playground, this light and refreshing libation is classically made with egg white to envelop all the flavors in an elegant froth. Whenever using egg white in a drink, tradition calls for it to be well-shaken for a few minutes to mix the ingredients and obtain the right amount of froth. Use raw egg at your discretion, or substitute pasteurized egg.

Shake all of the ingredients except the mint sprig vigorously with ice. Strain into a chilled cocktail glass or over ice in an old-fashioned glass. Garnish with the mint sprig.

1½ ounces light rum
½ ounce Cointreau
½ ounce fresh lime juice
1 egg white (optional)
½ ounce sugar syrup
(1 cup [235 ml] water and
1 cup [200 g]
granulated sugar)
Fresh mint sprig

Atlantic Breeze

THIS THIRST-QUENCHER contains all the elements of a great "breeze," with a floating whisper of anise, courtesy of the Galliano.

Pour all the liquid ingredients except the Galliano into an ice-filled highball glass. Stir briefly. Float the Galliano on top of the drink. Garnish with the orange slice.

1 1/2 ounces light rum
1/2 ounce apricot liqueur
1 1/2 ounces pineapple juice
1 1/2 ounces cranberry juice
1/2 ounce Galliano
Orange slice

My Mandarin from Havana

MY PREFERENCE FOR MANDARINS inspired this infusion of sweet mandarin flavor into a frozen Cuban-style daiquiri.

Combine all ingredients but the garnish with 1/2 cup ice in a blender. Blend until slushy. Using a fine-mesh metal strainer, slowly strain the mixture into a chilled cocktail glass. Float the lime wheel on top of the drink.

2 ounces silver rum
1 ounce Mandarine Napoléon liqueur
1 ounce fresh mandarin (or tangerine) juice
1/2 ounce fresh lime juice
1 teaspoon superfine sugar
1 thinly sliced lime wheel

Bossa Nova

THIS COCKTAIL CAME TO ME while I was throwing a Brasil '66 cocktail party. The guest of honor was, appropriately, cachaça, Brazil's favorite national spirit. Although they say you can power your Ford Fairlane with cachaça, I'd rather fuel a daiquiri with it myself. This version mixes rum's fiery cousin with the brandy-orange warmth of Cointreau, a splash of tangy cranberry, and the mellow hazelnut flavor of Frangelico for a surprising chocolate-like finish.

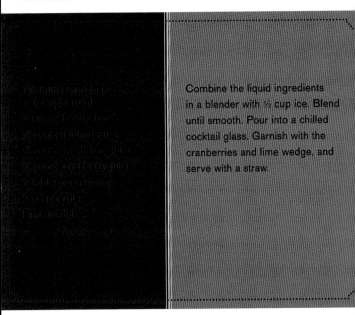

1½ ounces cachaça
  (or light rum)
½ ounce Frangelico
½ ounce Cointreau
½ ounce fresh lime juice
½ ounce cranberry juice
1 tablespoon honey
2 cranberries
lime wedge

Combine the liquid ingredients in a blender with ½ cup ice. Blend until smooth. Pour into a chilled cocktail glass. Garnish with the cranberries and lime wedge, and serve with a straw.

Pearl from Ipanema

TO CREATE A DRINK AS STYLISH as the Beauty on the Beach and as lively as Carnival, I combined Brazilian cachaça with sweet lime-flavored KeKe Beach liqueur and a refreshing splash of grapefruit, and arrived at this shimmering pink cocktail with pure liquid rhythm. For the best results, use true grenadine, which is made from pomegranates, not that ersatz bottled stuff that's colored red and sweetened with corn syrup.

Rub the rim of a chilled large cocktail glass with the lime wedge and rim with sugar. Shake the liquid ingredients vigorously with ice. Strain into the prepared glass. Twist the lime peel over the drink, and drop it in.

Lime wedge
Sugar, for rim
Cracked ice, plus
to fill drink
2 ounces cachaça
1 ounce KeKe Beach
lime liqueur
1 ounce grapefruit juice
1 tablespoon pomegranate
syrup (real grenadine)
Lime twist

sensual

· Luxurious yumminess for your mouth ·

Citrus Aphrodisiac

THE LEGENDARY DAMIANA LIQUEUR from Baja California, Mexico, is a sweet, flowery herbal liqueur that possesses a reputation as a powerful aphrodisiac. Seduced by the thought of conjuring up some sultry potion, I muddled around with the limey Caipirinha, coming up with this decadent, honeyed spin. The heady notes of Barbancourt rum and Damiana replace the traditional cachaça and warm up the fresh limes and tangerine juice. Such an elixir will indeed incite desire—at least for another.

Squeeze the lime wedges into a chilled double old-fashioned glass, and then drop in. Add the honey and Damiana, and muddle with the limes. Fill the glass with ice, and pour in the rum and tangerine juice. Stir briefly.

1 lime, quartered
1 tablespoon honey
1 ounce Damiana liqueur
1½ ounces Rhum Barbancourt
3 ounces fresh tangerine juice

· Variation · For a HAITIAN COOLER, add a few orange and lemon wedges to muddle, and top with ginger ale or spicy ginger beer.

Royal Palm Cocktail

FOR THOSE WHO DIG BANANAS, have I got the drink for you!
This sultry, vanilla-infused martini has just a whisper of banana—
99 Bananas, to be exact. Vanilla-infused rum is easy to make
and great to have on hand. Simply place a few long vanilla beans
in a bottle of silver or gold rum, and let stand for at least
a week—I actually leave the beans in the bottle indefinitely.

Coat the inside of a chilled cocktail
glass with the banana liqueur,
and discard any remaining liqueur.
Stir the vanilla-infused rum in a
mixing glass with ice. Strain into the
prepared glass and garnish with
the vanilla bean.

Cocoanut Groove

INSPIRED BY THE FAMOUS 1950S HOT SPOT THE COCOANUT GROVE, I imagined a signature house drink with lush island flavors designed to sate a suave clientele working up a thirst on the dance floor. This cocktail, reminiscent of Key lime pie made with coconut cream, would definitely qualify. Using coconut sorbet makes for a lighter, frostier drink, while rich, creamy coconut gelato turns it into a great after-dinner libation.

1 1/2 ounces Malibu (or other coconut-flavored rum)
1/2 cup coconut sorbet or gelato
1 ounce fresh lime juice
1 ounce coconut milk
1 ounce pineapple juice
Pineapple wedge
Dusting of ground nutmeg

Combine all ingredients but the garnishes in a blender with 1/2 cup ice. Blend until smooth. Pour into a chilled cocktail glass. Garnish with the pineapple, and sprinkle the top with nutmeg.

Copabanana Daiquiri

IN MY QUEST TO CONCOCT A SOPHISTICATED DAIQUIRI that would capture the magical ambiance of the legendary 1940s Copacabana Nightclub, where Latin sounds were enjoyed beneath swaying palm fronds—I came up with this velvety cocktail, where Island breeze meets urban savvy melding banana, raspberry, lime, and spiced rum.

Combine all ingredients but the garnishes in a blender with ½ cup ice. Blend until smooth. Pour into a chilled cocktail glass. Garnish with the raspberries and lime wheel.

Velvet Voodoo

SPELLBOUND BY THE BUTTERY, RICH TASTE of Rhum Barbancourt, my favorite Haitian rum, and the sounds of Screamin' Jay Hawkins crooning "I Put a Spell on You" in my head, I conjured up the perfect nightcap. Laced with amaretto and the infamous anise-flavored, chartreuse-hued absinthe (available as Absente), this creamy potion is full of powerful island magic.

Combine all the ingredients except the garnishes in a blender with ½ cup ice. Blend until smooth. Pour into a chilled cocktail glass. Dust the top with the nutmeg and sprinkle with a few chocolate shavings.

1½ ounces Rhum
Barbancourt
½ ounce Absente (Absinthe,
available with mint, such
as Pernod)
½ ounce amaretto
½ cup vanilla ice cream
Freshly grated or ground
nutmeg
Chocolate shavings

Tidal Wave

THE TROPICAL COCKTAIL GENRE is full of aquamarine concoctions evoking the shimmering waves. The challenge is to make one so fabulous that even the most jaded beachnik will want to sip it. My frothy, blue-hued elixir made with Malibu, the rum-based coconut-flavored liqueur from the Caribbean, and a wave of orange and almond flavors is so good, it will surely knock you right off your surfboard.

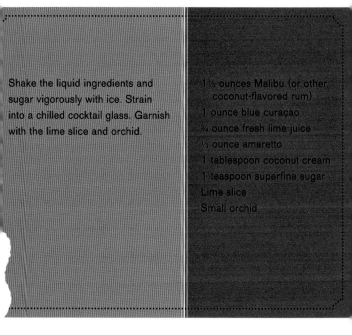

Shake the liquid ingredients and sugar vigorously with ice. Strain into a chilled cocktail glass. Garnish with the lime slice and orchid.

1½ ounces Malibu (or other coconut-flavored rum)

1 ounce blue curaçao

¾ ounce fresh lime juice

½ ounce amaretto

1 tablespoon coconut cream

1 teaspoon superfine sugar

Lime slice

Small orchid

Tiger's Milk

A RICH ELABORATION ON THE CLASSIC MILK PUNCH, Tiger's Milk blends the warm intensity of dark rum and brandy with cream and sugar for an enjoyable late-evening tipple. This eye-opener also comes in handy as a traditional hang-over remedy.

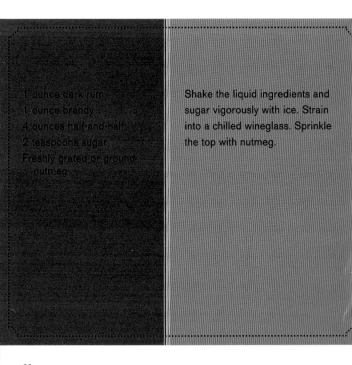

1 ounce dark rum
1 ounce brandy
4 ounces half-and-half
2 teaspoons sugar
Freshly grated or ground
  nutmeg

Shake the liquid ingredients and sugar vigorously with ice. Strain into a chilled wineglass. Sprinkle the top with nutmeg.

Tobago Coconut Flip

WHEN THE WINTER HOLIDAYS CALL FOR A BIT OF EXTRA WARMTH, I like to shake up a few of these frothy, festive numbers. Coconut-flavored Malibu rum is spiced up with an intriguing blend of rich coconut milk and Goldschläger, the Swiss cinnamon liqueur swirling with gold leaf, to send your palate on vacation to a remote Pacific island.

Shake the liquid ingredients vigorously with ice. Strain into a chilled cocktail glass. Sprinkle a dusting of cinnamon over the top, and float the orange blossom on the drink.

1½ ounces Malibu (or other coconut-flavored rum)
1 ounce Thai coconut milk
½ ounce Goldschläger (or other cinnamon schnapps)
Ground cinnamon
Orange blossom

· *stimulating* ·

· Caffeinated and fizzy drinks for a fun buzz ·

Jamaican Martini

THIS AROMATIC, SPICY COCKTAIL IS ENERGIZED by the rich island flavors of dark molasses and rum-based Tia Maria, which is made from Jamaican Blue Mountain coffee.

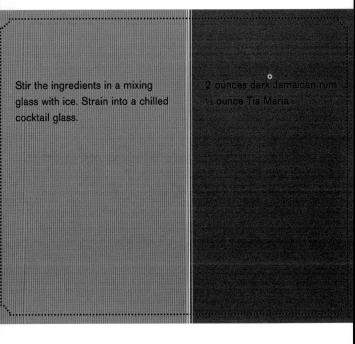

Stir the ingredients in a mixing glass with ice. Strain into a chilled cocktail glass.

2 ounces dark Jamaican rum
½ ounce Tia Maria

· Variation · For a KINGSTON COCKTAIL, add ¼ ounce fresh lime juice.

Dark and Stormy

THIS SPARKLING BERMUDA FAVORITE is a refreshing way to combat the heat as well as soothe the stomach. The smoky molasses tones of Gosling's black rum and the tangy bite of Jamaican ginger beer (similar to ginger ale but with a stronger ginger flavor) are spiced up with a fresh ginger kick.

Fill an old-fashioned glass with ice and add the fresh ginger, if desired. Add the rum and simple syrup, and stir. Top with ginger beer. Squeeze the lime wedges over the drink, and drop them in.

1 to 2 slices fresh ginger (optional)

2 ounces Gosling's Black Seal (or other dark rum)

1 tablespoon simple syrup (page 28) or superfine sugar

3 to 4 ounces chilled ginger beer

2 lime wedges

Honolulu Lulu

BATTEN DOWN THE LAMPSHADES AND HOIST UP THE CHANDELIERS. This is my Zombie-inspired hurricane in a glass, with a turbulent whirl of rums, fruity nectar, luscious liqueurs, and a zing of lime (see page 36). It's guaranteed to blow the roof off any civilized gathering. The drink is based on the traditional Hawaiian rules for rum punch: one part sour (citrus), two parts sweet (syrup or liqueur), three parts strong (rum), and four parts weak (juice).

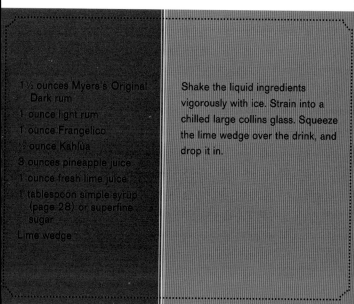

- 1½ ounces Myers's Original Dark rum
- 1 ounce light rum
- 1 ounce Frangelico
- ½ ounce Kahlúa
- 3 ounces pineapple juice
- 1 ounce fresh lime juice
- 1 tablespoon simple syrup (page 28) or superfine sugar
- Lime wedge

Shake the liquid ingredients vigorously with ice. Strain into a chilled large collins glass. Squeeze the lime wedge over the drink, and drop it in.

Old Cuban

OLD HAVANA MEETS URBAN SWANK in this elegant take on the Mojito, melding the classic combo of mint, lime, and rum with the suave effervescence of sparkling wine. This zippy champagne cocktail comes from Bemelman's Bar at the Carlyle Hotel in New York.

Shake the liquid ingredients and mint vigorously with ice. Strain into a chilled champagne flute. Slowly top with champagne, and stir gently. Garnish with the vanilla bean.

1½ ounces good-quality rum
¾ ounce fresh lime juice
Dash of Angostura bitters
1 ounce simple syrup (page 28) or 1 tablespoon superfine sugar
6 mint leaves
1½ ounces chilled champagne
Half a vanilla bean

Barracuda

A REFINED HINT OF ANISE FROM GALLIANO JOINS the potent tropical trio of rum, pineapple, and lime. Swept up in the effervescence of champagne, this sleek combination will have you circling back for a second.

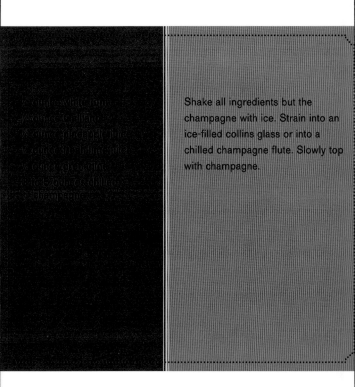

1½ ounces white rum
½ ounce Galliano
¾ ounce pineapple juice
½ ounce fresh lime juice
¼ ounce gin juice
ice to make to chilled
1 champagne

Shake all ingredients but the champagne with ice. Strain into an ice-filled collins glass or into a chilled champagne flute. Slowly top with champagne.

Jade

SHIMMERING, PALE-GREEN HINTS OF MINT AND ORANGE LIQUEUR whisper through this daiquiri-esque libation.

Shake the liquid ingredients and sugar vigorously with ice. Strain into a chilled cocktail glass. Float the lime slice on top of the drink.

1 ½ ounces light rum
½ teaspoon Cointreau
½ teaspoon green crème de menthe
¾ ounce fresh lime juice
1 teaspoon sugar
Thinly cut lime slice

Caribbean Fizz

THIS SPARKLING ELIXIR IS PURE ISLAND DECADENCE. With a lush combination of molasses-rich dark rum, fruity banana, and pineapple, it's surely the nectar of the Caribbean gods.

Shake all ingredients but the champagne vigorously with ice. Strain into a chilled champagne flute, and slowly top with champagne.

1 ounce dark rum
1 ounce banana purée
1 ounce pineapple juice
3 to 5 ounces chilled champagne

Index

Liquid Measurements

BAR SPOON	½ ounce
1 teaspoon	⅙ ounce
1 tablespoon	½ ounce
2 tablespoons (PONY)	1 ounce
3 tablespoons (JIGGER)	1½ ounces

¼ cup	2 ounces
⅓ cup	3 ounces
½ cup	4 ounces
⅔ cup	5 ounces
¾ cup	6 ounces
1 cup	8 ounces
1 pint	16 ounces
1 quart	32 ounces
750-ml bottle	25.4 ounces
1-liter bottle	33.8 ounces

1 medium lemon	3 tablespoons juice
1 medium lime	2 tablespoons juice
1 medium orange	⅓ cup juice